Stephen Leacock's Mariposa

Stephen Leacock's Mariposa

ONE HUNDRED YEARS OF SUNSHINE,
A WALKING TOUR OF ORILLIA

DAPHNE MAINPRIZE

Foreword by James A. "Pete" McGarvey
Introduction by Carl Spadoni

DUNDURN
TORONTO

Copyright © Daphne Mainprize, 2012

All rights reserved. No part of this publication may be reproduced, stored in a retrieval system, or transmitted in any form or by any means, electronic, mechanical, photocopying, recording, or otherwise (except for brief passages for purposes of review) without the prior permission of Dundurn Press. Permission to photocopy should be requested from Access Copyright.

Copy Editor: Allister Thompson
Design: Emma Dolan
Printer: Webcom

Library and Archives Canada Cataloguing in Publication

Mainprize, Daphne
   Stephen Leacock's Mariposa : one hundred years of
Sunshine, a walking tour of Orillia / Daphne Mainprize ;
foreword by James A. "Pete" McGarvey ; introduction by
Carl Spadoni.

Issued also in electronic format.
ISBN 978-1-4597-0759-7

   1. Leacock, Stephen, 1869-1944. 2. Leacock, Stephen,
1869-1944. Sunshine sketches of a little town. 3. Orillia
(Ont.)--In literature. I. Title.

PS8523.E15Z884 2012   C818'.5209   C2012-901427-3

1 2 3 4 5   16 15 14 13 12

Conseil des Arts du Canada   Canada Council for the Arts   Canadä   **ONTARIO ARTS COUNCIL CONSEIL DES ARTS DE L'ONTARIO**

We acknowledge the support of the **Canada Council for the Arts** and the **Ontario Arts Council** for our publishing program. We also acknowledge the financial support of the **Government of Canada** through the **Canada Book Fund** and **Livres Canada Books**, and the **Government of Ontario** through the **Ontario Book Publishing Tax Credit** and the **Ontario Media Development Corporation**.

Care has been taken to trace the ownership of copyright material used in this book. The author and the publisher welcome any information enabling them to rectify any references or credits in subsequent editions.

J. Kirk Howard, President

Printed and bound in Canada.
www.dundurn.com

Dundurn	Gazelle Book Services Limited	Dundurn
3 Church Street, Suite 500	White Cross Mills	2250 Military Road
Toronto, Ontario, Canada	High Town, Lancaster, England	Tonawanda, NY
M5E 1M2	LA1 4XS	U.S.A. 14150

In memory of

Jay Cody (1922–2011)
Curator Emeritus, Stephen Leacock Museum

Wilma Patterson (1923–2011)

A portion of the author's
royalties for this book will support
the Stephen Leacock Museum
National Historic Site

Contents

Foreword   9
by James A. "Pete" McGarvey

Introduction   17
Orillia and Mariposa in Leacock's
Sunshine Sketches of a Little Town
by Carl Spadoni

Acknowledgements   29

Chapter One   31
Mariposa: The Beginnings

Chapter Two   41
Along the Shoreline: Historic Landmarks

Chapter Three   52
The *Sketches*: The Cast of Characters
in Leacock's Mariposa

Chapter Four   81
Mariposa Citizens Today

Chapter Five   96
Stephen Leacock Museum
National Historic Site
by Fred Addis

Chapter Six The Walking Tour of Stephen Leacock's Mariposa	100
Historic Map of Leacock's Mariposa	105
Sources	106
Websites of Interest	108

Foreword

Happy hundredth birthday, Mariposa! Let the cannons roar, the rockets ascend, the bells peal!

It's been quite a ride!

What was at first perceived to be a gentle josh at the dreams and schemes of the citizens of a typical Ontario town (pre–First World War) is now recognized as Stephen Leacock's masterpiece, and adjudged by some critics as the most important book about Canada and Canadians by a Canadian writer since Confederation.

Though the McGill professor insisted that he had no particular municipality in mind, no Orillians were fooled. People, events, and sites were all unmistakably Orillian. Who else could mortician Golgotha Gingham be but Orillia's Horace Bingham; St. James' Anglican Church was obviously the "beacon on the hill"; and Netley's Store on Missanabi Street could be none other than Hatley's Market on Mississaga Street.

The *Sketches* were Leacock's third volume of humour. The first, *Literary Lapses*, appeared in 1910, when Leacock headed the Department of Economics and Political Science at Montreal's McGill University.

He had already attained much acclaim for his seminal work, *Elements of Economics*, published in 1906. When word got out that he was preparing to publish a book of humorous essays composed a decade earlier for New York magazines, his colleagues encouraged him to banish the idea. He was told that he could be either a serious learned professor or a buffoon, but surely not both.

Leacock knew better. He felt entirely at home in both fields and proved it over and over again in the decades to come, much to the world's benefit.

The *Sketches*, critically, got off to a bad start when one reporter canvassed a number of Orillians on their reaction to the book, which led to a sensational account of Leacock maligning the gentle and decent folk of Orillia for cheap laughs. The impression lasted for many decades, usually beginning with the words "Orillians will never forgive Stephen Leacock for his cheap caricaturing of his neighbors in the *Sketches*."

I knew all about Mariposa from grade six onward. I recall rushing home from school to regale my parents with a story of a steamboat that floundered and sank all of one foot. And the rescuers, who turned up in various craft, had to be themselves rescued. The author was one Stephen Leacock.

My dad murmured, "I knew the man," and indeed he did. He spent a year in Orillia in 1905, at the Tudhope Carriage Works, and boarded with a cousin of Leacock's closest Orillia pal, Charlie Janes. There was no question that he had encountered the famed humorist some years before Leacock achieved world acclaim.

Foreword

I arrived in Orillia in mid-April 1947, hired as a commercial writer for the local radio station, CFOR. In the several hours before my interview, I toured the main streets, gaped at the Opera House, and visited Couchiching Beach Park, and to my amazement found absolutely no reference to Mariposa — no Stephen Leacock Park, or street, school, or historic plaque. The people I met could offer no information whatsoever on *Sunshine Sketches*, Mariposa, or the humorist behind them. Many appeared not to care, and none was sure where his summer home was, or had been — somewhere on Lake Couchiching's shore.

Three months later, I was asked by the program director to attend a banquet honouring Leacock with the presentation of the very first Leacock Medal of Humour. My resume stated that I was widely experienced in interviewing but neglected to mention that all had been written interviews to be used by broadcasters. I had never held a microphone in my life, and I was sure I would be found out, but the dinner on Friday, June 13, at Orchard Point Inn, was a royal feast of non-stop laughter, with former literary friends and Orillia comrades recalling the antics and hospitality of the genuine genius of Canadian humour.

My inhibitions melted and I faced the principals of the function unafraid. I still have those direct-to-disk 78 rpm recordings from "the night that changed my life forever." I can remember the precise words of publisher, author, and critic B.K. Sandwell. He said, "Stephen Leacock taught me French at Upper Canada College, in

(I hate to say) 1891. He was a *good* teacher, and we boys all knew that he was writing articles for New York funny papers, which he would read from time to time to our delight. But he never let that interfere with his teaching."

I met Charles Harold Hale that night — the publisher of the Orillia *Packet* for half a century, and a close friend of Leacock's for the same number of years. I knew him by reputation as the driving force for moulding Orillia into the foremost town in Canada — proud of its history, and forward-looking. I expected a dynamic figure but could scarcely believe that so much local fervor stemmed from this mild-mannered, soft-spoken, elderly gentleman.

I resolved that night that if I were to remain in Orillia, I would join this body of enthusiasts and try to, if possible, repatriate its neglected Leacock legacy.

I was nineteen at the time, but before I reached my thirtieth birthday, joined with Harold Hale as my mentor, partner, and treasured friend, I would see the fulfillment of that resolve (my account of this grand venture is contained in *The Old Brewery Bay*, published by Dundurn Press in 1994).

In the years following publication of the *Sketches*, it became a global sensation, translated into a score of languages, including Russian, Chinese, Japanese, French, German, and Hungarian. After the opening of the Stephen Leacock Museum National Historic Site in July 1958, hundreds of our visitors told of their discovery of the book and its influence upon them.

In Toronto some years ago, I befriended George Jonas, who had escaped Budapest during the communist crackdown in the spring of 1956. He told me he had three possible safe havens — in France, the United States, and Canada. His decision in favour of Canada owed everything to his delight in reading the *Sketches*. If that's what Canadians are like, he reasoned, that's where I want to be.

The book has gone everywhere, including to a tiny island called Réunion, 280 miles southeast of Madagascar. In the early nineties, I received a letter from Paris-born Maxime Aubry. In the daytime, Maxime taught French. Evenings and weekends were devoted to patiently translating the works of Stephen Leacock into French. Yearly leaves were devoted to searching out Leacock lore in England and the United States. In 1997, he arrived in Orillia. It was an emotional encounter. He haunted the museum for three days and on the Sunday of that week was conducted to many of the sites found in *Sunshine Sketches*. We drove to the country crossroads of Egypt, to the remnants of the farm the Leacock family moved to in 1876. The visit wound up at Upper Canada College in Toronto, where, to our amazement, there appeared to be little material relating to Leacock's tenure as both a student and teacher. When Maxime departed for Montreal that evening by train, it struck home just how globally the genius of Leacock stretched.

In the fifty-four years since the museum opened, it has known only five curators, each contributing greatly to Leacock lore and the Orillia–Mariposa context. First came Doctor Ralph Curry from Kentucky, the pre-eminent Leacock scholar of his time, who knew precisely what should be recognized in a museum bearing Leacock's name — his brilliance as a world-renowned humorist, his life as an acclaimed economist, historian, lecturer, and, above all else, the creation of Mariposa in *Sunshine Sketches*.

Ralph was succeeded in 1973 by Orillia historian Jay Cody, whose tenure emphasized the Orillia–Mariposa linkage. He assembled the Mariposa room, consisting of relics of Orillia's 1912 — pictures and artifacts, which included the barbershop pole from Jeff Shortt's shop. Jay also organized sailing regattas, cricket matches, lawn bowling, and croquet, which were favourite summer pastimes in Leacock's day.

Daphne Mainprize, who began as Jay's understudy in 1991 and was installed as curator in 1995, is eminently qualified to guide visitors through the museum and to the Orillia sites from the *Sketches*. During her tenure, Daphne presided over the construction of Swanmore Hall, the visitor centre, the successful campaign to designate The Old Brewery Bay as a national historic site, and the volunteer effort to rebuild the Leacock boathouse.

The close of the twentieth century found the museum in a battle with city hall over the matter of governance. Daphne came on like a mother bear protecting her cubs. She starred in David Langer's brilliant 1998 CBC production *The Life and Times of Stephen Leacock*, and a year later co-authored with me *The Stephen Leacock Picture Book* (another Dundurn publication).

Her successors in the twenty-first century, Craig Metcalf and Fred Addis, have made the museum a true

FOREWORD

gathering place for outstanding Canadian writers and have created programs to acquaint school children with the mirth and wisdom of the Baron of Brewery Bay.

In his long, productive lifetime, Stepehen Leacock was acclaimed in all quarters of the Earth and reaped the financial rewards of his many volumes. His literary compatriots heaped accolades upon him. J.B. Priestley wrote, "Canada should not only be proud of Stephen Leacock, but specially grateful to him. The best of his humour does something very difficult to do — it expresses an essential Canadian quality. He achieves an outlook, manner, style that typical British and American humorists find impossible to achieve. These belong to the man but they also belong to his nation." Amen.

Please explore with Daphne's guide in hand the true sites and wonders that inspired a truly unique Canadian.

JAMES A. "PETE" MCGARVEY
Founder, Stephen Leacock National Historic Site,
Orillia, Ontario
March 2012

Introduction
Orillia and Mariposa in Leacock's *Sunshine Sketches of a Little Town*

Written by Stephen Leacock, Canada's greatest humorist, *Sunshine Sketches of a Little Town* is an affectionate satire of small town life and local politics in Ontario prior to the First World War. The narrator of this pastoral comedy is at once simple-minded and sophisticated. The stories such as the sinking of the *Mariposa Belle*, the burning of the Church of England church, the convoluted romance between Peter Pupkin and Zena Pepperleigh, and the great election in Missinaba County, are hilarious, endearing, nostalgic, and wistful. Published a century ago in 1912, *Sunshine Sketches* first appeared serially in twelve installments in the *Montreal Star* between February 17 and June 12, and then in book form under the imprint of John Lane, The Bodley Head, in England on August 9, with simultaneous publication in the United States and Canada a month later on September 20. The book sold quite well during Leacock's lifetime (43,000 copies), which by Canadian standards in publishing of its day constitutes a minor miracle.

Even more miraculous is the fact that the book has remained in print in many editions and continues to sell briskly to new generations of readers. When McClelland & Stewart, for example, inaugurated the New Canadian Library paperback series in 1958, Leacock proved to be one of the most popular authors in the series, and *Sunshine Sketches* sold 142,325 copies between 1960 (the year of the NCL publication) and 1979. Online versions of *Sunshine Sketches* can be found on the web at the Literature Network, Project Gutenberg, Google Books, and iTunes. *Sunshine Sketches* is a Canadian classic. It belongs on the same bookshelf as two other extraordinary Canadian bestsellers of the same era: Robert W. Service's *Songs of a Sourdough* (1907) and L.M. Montgomery's *Anne of Green Gables* (1908).

With his tongue firmly planted in his cheek, Professor Stephen Leacock, dubbed the Canadian Mark Twain by his publishers, wrote the following in the preface to *Sunshine Sketches of a Little Town*: "In regard to the present work I must disclaim at once all intention of trying to do anything so ridiculously easy as writing about a real place and real people." All fiction, one can argue, no matter how imaginatively written, is ultimately a mirror, a prism, a distillation, or a diluted expression of an author's upbringing, education, experience, and opinions. But in his preface Leacock coyly persisted in his denial of any intended attribution to real characters, places, and events.

With respect to Mariposa, the book's fictional setting on the shores of Lake Wissanotti in Missinaba County, he maintained that it was not an actual town but a composite of seventy or eighty towns located in

Canada "from Lake Superior to the sea," where one could find the same streets, maple trees, churches, and hotels. He extended this line of explanation to the book's cast of lovable characters. The Reverend Mr. Rupert Drone, Henry Mullins, John Henry Bagshaw, Judge Pepperleigh, Peter Pupkin, Jos. Smith ... yes, he was personally acquainted with all of them, but they were composites he had encountered at different times and in many places. What should not be forgotten, Leacock reminded his readers, was the inspiration of *Sunshine Sketches*, "a land of hope and sunshine" where ordinary people, in spite of their foibles, adversities, and misadventures, are basically good and content citizens in a community with shared values.

Leacock's disclaimer in his preface did not fool many Canadian reviewers of his book. In Orillia, Ontario, where Leacock lived at Old Brewery Bay during the summer when he was not teaching political economy at McGill University in Montreal, there was no doubt as to the source of his inspiration. The anonymous reviewer in the *Orillia News Packet* (December 12, 1912, page 3) stated:

> For despite the author's denial that he had in mind any town in particular, the belief will not down that he caught much of the inspiration for his Sketches in the "little town" where he has spent his leisure for the past fifteen years, and where he has known the idiosyncrasies of so many of the people. We fear that

> no amount of asseveration on Dr. Leacock's part will convince Orillians that they do not "recognize" some of the characters. This is, in truth the highest praise his book can have, for it shows that, under the exaggeration of the humour, it is true to life. But while many of the allusions have a familiar ring, Dr. Leacock has not been guilty of paragraphing individuals, and there is no room for resentment, in fact Orillians are rather proud to think that Orillia is the "little town," which has been immortalized as a type of Canadian life.

Mariposa was certainly Orillia, Lake Wissanotti was Lake Couchiching, and Jefferson Thorpe was Jeff Shortt, whose barbershop was located in the Syndicate Block on Mississaga Street East. These are but a few examples of the many documented attributions that can be found in *Sunshine Sketches*. The surviving draft tables of contents of the book and the sporadic comments made by Leacock himself (when he let his satirical mask slip) clearly substantiate that he based much of *Sunshine Sketches* on people, places, and events in Orillia and its environs.

Non-residents of Orillia, including notable commentators such as William Arthur Deacon, Hector Charlesworth, Robertson Davies, and Margaret Macmillan, have wrongly conjectured that *Sunshine Sketches* greatly offended the townsfolk of Orillia. Leacock's own mother, Agnes Leacock, it has been alleged, even scolded him for his caricature of Canon Richard W. Greene, the rector of St. James' Anglican Church. An article in *Maclean's* magazine ("Soaking Up the Sunshine," February 6, 1912, pages 50–51, by Nicholas Köhler) perpetuates the myth that "for decades, the residents of Orillia resented Stephen Leacock for skewering them in his popular stories." In point of fact, during Leacock's lifetime, the majority of Orillians remained blissfully ignorant of Leacock's international stature as a humorist and social pundit. Selling his produce to the local market, Leacock looked more like a gentleman farmer than a famous author or a professor. He was not one to parade his learning or to mock in a blatant way the lack of culture in his hometown. At Orillia, when not writing, he entertained family and friends and took pleasure in gardening, sailing, and fishing. For his part, Leacock loved Orillia with an enduring fondness.

Although academic, literary critics have routinely refused to regard *Sunshine Sketches* as a true novel and have labelled the book with a number of baffling terms (a near-novel, a proto-novel, a para-novel, a short-story ensemble, a series of vignettes, etc.), *Sunshine Sketches* is a veritable *roman à clef*. This French phrase, which translates as "novel with a key," refers to a work of fiction in which the author employs made-up names and places for their respective real counterparts. The literary genre of the *roman à clef* goes back to the seventeenth century, when writers necessarily disguised their criticisms of government and scandals in society by resorting to fiction, thus avoiding self-incrimination or the incrimination of others. Famous works of literature such as H.G. Wells's *Ann Veronica* (1909), Ernest Hemingway's *The Sun Also Rises* (1926), and F. Scott Fitzgerald's *Tender Is the Night* (1934) are often cited as examples of *roman à clef*. *Sunshine Sketches* belongs to this same rich literary tradition of disguised satire.

The extent of Leacock's fictional depiction in *Sunshine Sketches* of people and places in Orillia has been documented in the critical edition of the novel published by Broadview Press in 2002. I had the privilege and honour of editing the Broadview edition. In addition to Leacock's text of *Sunshine Sketches*, the Broadview edition includes a detailed introduction, explanatory annotations, contemporary reviews, lists of textual variants in the serialization in the *Montreal Star* and the extant manuscript, and a range of contextual materials such as Leacock's stage adaptation of *Sunshine Sketches*. The introduction has a section entitled "Orillia and Mariposa," and there is an appendix of attributions. Two of the major storylines in *Sunshine Sketches*, for example, the sinking of the *Mariposa Belle* and the burning of the Church of England church, have parallels to and linkages with events in Orillia history, respectively: the sinking of the twin-screw steamer *Enterprise* in the summer of 1902 on Lake Simcoe, when it docked at the Mulcaster Street wharf in Barrie and was found sitting on the bottom the next morning; and the fire at St. James' Anglican Church in Orillia on 19 March 1905, which spread rapidly on a Sunday morning, leaving behind a ragged group of walls, a sodden heap of bricks, and blackened wood.

Notwithstanding obvious similarities between fact and fiction, it would be a mistake to assume that every aspect of Orillia's life and culture is mirrored in Leacock's Mariposa. At least two of the stories in *Sunshine Sketches* have no apparent connection to Orillia: the whirlwind campaign to reduce the debt of the Church of England church; and the Mariposa bank mystery. The real whirlwind campaign took place at Leacock's own university in November and December 1911. McGill University had incurred a series of deficits, caused in part by expansion and losses through fire.

In *Sunshine Sketches*, Peter Pupkin, the lovelorn bank clerk, contemplates suicide when he sees Zena Pepperleigh dancing with another man at the Firemen's Ball. Pupkin and the bank's caretaker discharge their revolvers when they mistake one another for an armed bank robber. A similar incident but without romantic entanglements was reported in the Toronto *Globe* on May 22, 1895. In the Dominion Bank, E. Homer Dixon accidentally discharged a teller's revolver and almost killed himself. Like Pupkin, who was initially in grave mortal peril, Dixon's condition gradually improved (see D.M.R. Bentley, "Rummagings 2: Stephen Leacock" at *http://canadianpoetry.org/volumes/vol53/preface.html*).

The Stephen Leacock Museum, a national historic site, is a cultural mecca that attracts thousands of visitors annually. On the property one can find Swanmore Hall, an archival and visitor centre with a gift shop and café, and Leacock's reconstructed boathouse on the shoreline. The museum offers educational and outreach programs for children, readings, literary festivals, and writers' workshops. One can even follow in the footsteps of Peter Pupkin and Zena Pepperleigh and be married on the Leacock estate.

This is Stephen Leacock's dream and his legacy to Orillia. The museum has undergone a radical transformation since the purchase of the property by Leacock in 1908 and the construction of his stately house in 1928, designed by the Toronto architectural firm Wright and Noxon. But this idyllic setting on Old Brewery Bay experienced a turbulent period after Leacock's death. When Pete McGarvey, the author of *The Old Brewery Bay: A Leacockian Tale* (1994), saw the property in 1949, it was in a state of disrepair, bordering on ruin: "There were shattered windows, sagging shutters, a roof that leaked, weed-choked lawns and gardens, and mustiness, decay and neglect everywhere," he recalls (page 24).

The Stephen Leacock Associates was established in 1946 to preserve and to promote Leacock's legacy and to encourage the growth of Canadian humorous writing. Under its auspices, the Stephen Leacock Memorial Medal for Humour has been awarded annually to great fanfare.

In spite of the praiseworthy work of the Leacock Associates, Leacock's home went into decline in the 1950s. McGarvey and other heroic local citizens such as

INTRODUCTION

C. Harold Hale (the publisher of the Orillia *Packet Times*, whose family newspaper appears in *Sunshine Sketches* as the *Newspacket*) were determined visionaries. Initially, their view was in the minority, yet they prevailed and wrested control of Leacock's property for the public good. When I first visited the Leacock Museum thirty years ago in 1982, seventy years after the publication of *Sunshine Sketches*, I was enchanted by Leacock's house overlooking Lake Couchiching — the Mariposa room on the second floor with the original red, white, and blue pole from Shortt's barbershop and Horace Bingham's long black coat that he wore at funerals.

I arrived during a rainstorm on a hot summer's day and was greeted enthusiastically by Ralph Curry, the author of *Stephen Leacock: Humorist and Humanist* (1959) and the first curator of the museum, and by Jay Cody, Curry's curatorial successor. In those glorious days of my research when I explored and described Leacock's publishing history, I was left alone in Leacock's house after closing time, drank homemade beer from the museum's fridge, and set the alarm at midnight before leaving exhilarated and exhausted to a nearby hotel or a bed and breakfast. In the 1990s I had the pleasure of meeting Daphne Mainprize, an energetic curator and a tireless advocate of Leacock's comic genius and contribution to Canadian culture. The tradition of curatorial dedication at the Leacock Museum continues in the present day under Fred Addis.

Orillia is no longer the Sunshine town, once a quaint village, according to Leacock, "beside placid lakes almost within echo of the primeval forest." It is now the Sunshine city with a population in excess of 30,000 people. Economic activity takes in a mix of manufacturing, government services, customer service, and tourism. The largest employer is Casino Rama. There are two post-secondary institutions, being satellite campuses of Georgian College and Lakehead University. At times over the last fifty years since the establishment of the Stephen Leacock Museum, relations between Orillia and the Leacock Museum have been strained financially. For many years Orillia exploited the Leacock Museum by selling off lots of the Leacock estate to real estate developers. To a great extent those difficult days have passed, and there is an air of equanimity and an understanding of joint purpose between the city and the Leacock Museum. City council restricts the construction of large buildings downtown and seeks to maintain a "small town" look. Many local businesses use "Mariposa" in their names. It is now chic in Orillia to be associated with Stephen Leacock.

In 2012 we celebrate the hundredth anniversary of the publication of *Sunshine Sketches of a Little Town*. CBC has recently aired an adaptation of *Sunshine Sketches* in which the veteran actor Gordon Pinsent plays the part of Leacock's persona as narrator and author. To mark the occasion of the 2012 anniversary, Orillia will be hosting a Sunshine City Festival with horse and buggy rides and antique cars, live music and theatre, a heritage carnival, and a display at Couchiching Beach Park and on the waterfront. In his heyday Leacock wrote frothy short stories and serious articles for the popular press on both sides of the Atlantic. He spoke frequently on the lecture circuit and published one or two books a year. *Sunshine Sketches* remains his most popular book, a fictional tribute to his hometown of Orillia that he loved so well. Leacock has finally come home to Mariposa

CARL SPADONI
February 2012

Acknowledgements

Thanks to the following:

James A. "Pete" McGarvey, *Doctor of Humane Letters, honoris causa*, the *keeper* of the Leacock legacy, historian, author, founder of the Stephen Leacock Museum National Historic Site, and an exceptional person who has inspired so many of us to continue promoting the life, times, and works of Stephen Leacock, for writing the foreword. Pete authored *The Old Brewery Bay: A Leacockian Tale* (Dundurn Press, 1994) and in 1998 he and I co-authored *The Leacock Picture Book* (Dundurn Press, 1998).

Dr. Carl Spadoni, Director of the William Ready Division of Archives and Research Collections, McMaster University Library, for the introduction. As one of Canada's most prominent Leacock scholars, Carl has written extensively about the life and works of Stephen Leacock. In 1998, Carl completed *A Bibliography of Stephen Leacock* (ECW Press), which catalogues Leacock's works, and the critical edition of *Sunshine Sketches of a Little Town* (Broadview Press, 2002).

Fred Addis, Curator of the Stephen Leacock Museum National Historic Site, for access to the archives and for his assistance.

The Orillia Public Library, particularly Darcy Yanni

and the staff at the information services desk. Anne Di Tommaso for her collaboration with editing, logistics, and preparing the historic map graphics. Craig Mainprize for providing original illustrations for the book and his thoughtful input. John Rolland for bringing to life the stories of Mariposa and providing historic pictures of the waterfront.

At the Orillia Museum of Art and History for research and information, Wendy Hutchings and Marcel Rousseau.

Wib and Jean French for their stories of Mariposa and for their hospitality. Ralph Cipolla for his insight into the history of downtown Orillia. Tiffin's Creative Centre for their help with the photographs. Mundell Funeral Home for providing historic photos of the McCosh house. Also, thanks to John and Jody Waugh.

Mariposa Citizens Today, for their comments on the impact Stephen Leacock had on Orillia in the past hundred years and the future of his legacy in Mariposa: Reverend Terry Bennett, Steve Clarke, Doug Downey, Mark Fletcher, Tom Gostick, John Hammill, and Mayor Angelo Orsi.

Kirk Howard and the staff of Dundurn Press, particularly Allister Thompson.

Alexander for his patience.

Dale Duncan for providing her artwork of French's Food Stand.

The primary editions of *Sunshine Sketches of a Little Town* referenced for this book are the 1960 edition by McClelland & Stewart in the New Canadian Library, and the 2002 edition by Broadview Press, edited by Carl Spadoni.

Chapter One
Mariposa: The Beginnings

In 1912, the Town of Orillia was evolving into a vibrant, industrious place. Orillia at that time could be described as a frontier town, a lumber town, an industrial base, and a hub of cultural activity. This describes most of the small towns in Ontario during that time, but the average citizen of what was to become Mariposa saw things much differently. The people of Orillia had a well-defined sense of self and were an enterprising group that believed the town had it all. They were right to hold Orillia in such high regard. Only the "lands between" divided Orillia from the far north, where vast forests of high pines and bush fed the lumber industry. Hugged between the shorelines of Lake Simcoe and Lake Couchiching, Orillia enjoyed the vast opportunities that came with this strategic, geographic placement.

At the same time, the town was a breath away from cosmopolitan Toronto and provided a mecca for the city's weary people, who flocked to Orillia in search of the tranquillity that can only be found in places like Mariposa. However, the history of Orillia reaches much further into the past.

The story of Orillia goes back thousands of years. Over 4,500 years ago, the Huron Nation had a substantial settlement here. An estimated 30,000 Huron people lived along the shores of Lakes Simcoe and Couchiching. The place known as The Narrows is where the two lakes meet. The Huron people developed an innovative method of trapping fish, which has become known as "fish weirs," and was a stable source of food for the Huron people. This sacred location was known as an annual gathering place for First Nations from across northeast Canada and the eastern United States, and is near what is presently the Stephen Leacock Museum.

Sketch of the fish weirs at The Narrows. (Courtesy of Craig Mainprize)

Mariposa: The Beginnings

In 1615, Samuel de Champlain travelled to Cahiague region, which would eventually become Orillia and area. The experiences of Champlain and his fellow explorers in this area are well documented.

Champlain's travels and exploration throughout this region had a lasting impact not only on Orillia, but on the surrounding region. A bronze monument commemorating Champlain is located in Couchiching Park. As a member of the committee responsible for the proposed unveiling of the monument, in 1915 Stephen Leacock wrote to W.D. Lighthall (1857–1954), inviting him to write and read a poem at the unveiling ceremony. The idea for the monument originated with C.H. Hale and was created by Vernon March. Due to the First World War, the monument was not unveiled until 1925.

The Narrows with a view of the swing bridge and boathouses. (Leacock Museum Archives)

The Samuel de Champlain Monument. C.H. Hale stands beside the bronze statue of Champlain at Goddendene, Farnborough, U.K. (Orillia Public Library)

Stephen Leacock was first introduced to Orillia in 1895 by his mother, Agnes Leacock, who spent her summers on the shores of Lake Couchiching. Thus began Leacock's introduction to Orillia. His love affair with the town only grew with the years, and in 1907 he wrote his mother from the Grand Hotel de Genève, saying:

> Tell Charlie I am awfully anxious to get a place; if the little point is not too wet I'd like it. If it is not obtainable then the Hughes point. On either of those, he may, subject to ratification by me make an offer. And I'd like him to try & do something about it this summer so that I can take up the place next spring. The more I see of "foreign parts" the less I think of them compared with Canada. And I want a place of my own.

And there began the story that is Mariposa. He got that piece of property and made it his own, just as he made Orillia his own.

Stephen Leacock's decision to buy the piece of land that is today known as "The Old Brewery Bay" marked the beginning of the transformation of Orillia into Mariposa. In 1908 Stephen took up ownership of his land. Mariposa awakened and with it the Canadian identity, as defined in the pages of *Sunshine Sketches of a Little Town*.

Legions of readers over the last hundred years have imagined Mariposa, a sunny place on the shores of Lake Wissanotti (inspired by Lake Couchiching), taking comfort in the characters Leacock depicted. Perhaps they saw a bit of themselves appreciating the writer's ability to create a place that is worth going home to ... Mariposa!

Wharf and bay, Orillia at the turn of the century. (Courtesy of John Rolland)

One Hundred Years of Sunshine takes you on a nostalgic journey through Leacock's Mariposa, allowing you to capture the essence that inspired Leacock while experiencing the Mariposa of today.

Orillia from the air showing Lakes Simcoe and Couchiching. (Orillia Public Library)

MARIPOSA: THE BEGINNINGS

The Narrows, near Orillia, in the area of the fish weirs. (Orillia Public Library)

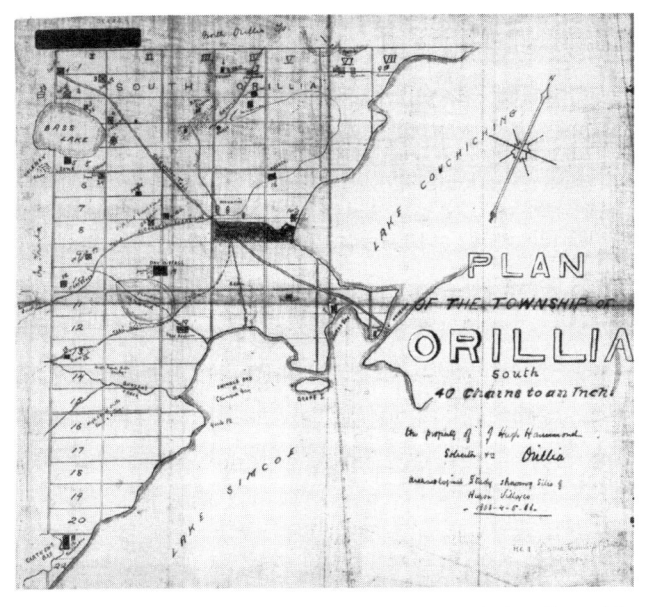

Archaeological sites of Huron villages, Orillia South. (Orillia Public Library)

On February 21, 1912, the Orillia *News Letter* published an article extolling the many fine qualities of Orillia. The picture painted in the article is of a thriving, vibrant, exciting place to be.

Things to Know About Orillia

- Orillia is the best town in Ontario
- Orillia has a fine General Hospital
- Orillia's population is now estimated at over 7,000
- Orillia is fast becoming a great railway centre
- In the matter of railways Orillia in a short time will be the best served town in Canada
- Orillia has a splendid sewerage system
- Orillia is the prettiest town in Ontario
- Orillia, the Interlaken city, is situated between Lake Simcoe and Lake Couchiching
- Orillia is one of the finest residential towns in Ontario
- Orillia is not only a beautiful town, but a healthy one
- "Couchiching Beach," Orillia's beautiful park, is one of the finest in the province and many excursions visit it annually
- Orillia is a manufacturing town, over 1,200 men working in factories located here
- Orillia is on the Trent Canal waterway, one of the scenic summer routes of the province which will soon become very popular with tourists
- Orillia's debenture debt is $617,172. Of this amount $386,341 is revenue producing
- In Municipal ownership Orillia is the most advanced town in Ontario

Mariposa: The Beginnings

- Orillia owns and operates its electric light and power house and water works systems
- Orillia has a splendid Public Library containing over 6,000 books
- Orillia has a good curling rink and club that is well-known throughout the province
- Orillia has the largest skating rink in Northern Ontario
- Orillia has the largest and best equipped Y.M.C.A of any town in America
- Orillia post office receipts last year amounted to $19,751
- The customs receipts at Orillia of last year amounted to $88.189 an increase of $38,000 over the previous year
- 621,953 dollars were paid by Orillia factories to their employees last year in wages
- Orillia factories turn out products to the value of $3,782,500 in 1911
- A new armoury to cost $60,000 is to be built in Orillia this year
- Orillia's first four-story block is now under construction
- There are 605 telephones in Orillia
- Orillia was incorporated as a town in 1875 with a population of 2,186
- Orillia gets its water supply for natural springs, which supply 250,000 gallons daily
- Orillia has a first-class opera house
- Orillia has a splendid fire alarm system

- Orillia, the home of champions, is one of the best known sporting towns in Canada

- The first white man to visit Orillia was Samuel de Champlain, the famous French explorer, who passed through the Narrows here in 1615

- There are four banks in Orillia, the Dominion, Traders, Merchants and Union

- Orillia has three Public Schools, one Separate School and a Collegiate Institute

- The religious institutions in Orillia include the Methodist church, Presbyterian church, Roman Catholic church, St. James' church, Baptist church, Salvation Army barracks and Gospel Hall

- The factories in Orillia manufacture automobiles, carriages, buggies, cutters, sleighs, sawmill, machinery, furniture, locks, flooring, clothing, plows, disc harrows, wagons, curtain poles, broom handles, baskets, doors, windows, frames, lumber, leather and other things

- There are three newspapers in Orillia

- Orillia's assessment is over $300,000

- Orillia is a great summer town and is visited by many tourists annually

- Orillia is served by three trans-continental railways, the CPR, GTR and CNR

- There are 100 private owned launches in Orillia and over 300 private owned canoes, rowboats and sailboats, besides three first-class boat liveries (*The News Letter*, February 21, 1912, page 1)

Chapter Two
Along the Shoreline: Historic Landmarks

The Rails

By 1912, the Town of Orillia was served by three transcontinental railways: the Canadian Pacific Railway (CPR); the Canadian National Railway (CNR); and the Grand Truck Railway (GTR). The shoreline of Orillia looked vastly different with the waterfront intersected by rail beds. Various companies servicing the rail and lumber industry scattered the waterfront.

The following pictures show the various activities that took place at the waterfront of Orillia.

An old postcard showing Couchiching Park. (Leacock Museum Archives)

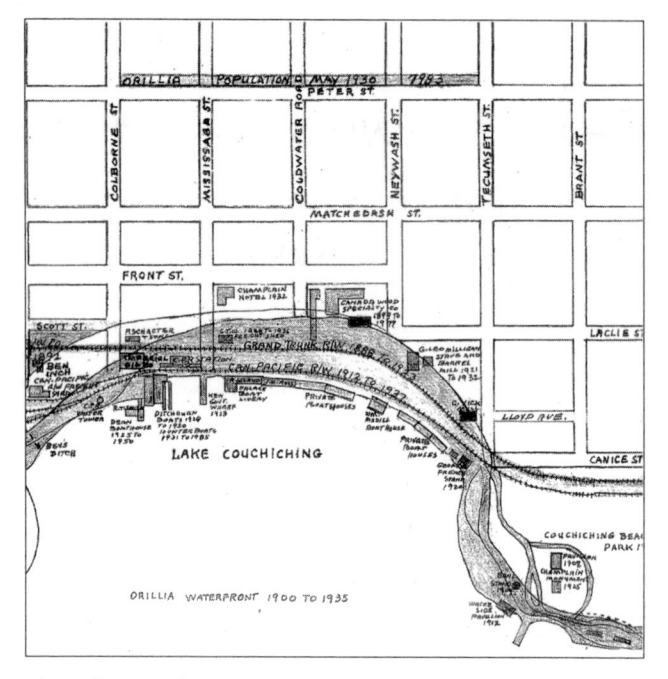

The Orillia waterfront with a view of the Grand Trunk Railway and the Canadian Pacific Railway from 1900 to 1935. (Courtesy of John Rolland)

The Orillia wharves showing the refreshment stand. (Orillia Public Library)

ALONG THE SHORELINE: HISTORICAL LANDMARKS

The 419 train to Mariposa. (Orillia Public Library)

In the midst of a bustling lumber and freight industry, the citizens of Orillia were enjoying the offerings that Lake Couchiching presented. The *Enterprise* and *Islay* boats plied the lakes, providing leisure excursions and shipping goods.

BOATS, LAKES, AND SHORELINES

Several boat and livery services had been long established along the waterfront. Stephen Leacock dealt with a number of these livery services but generally favoured Rolland Palace Boat Livery when he needed a boat to go fishing. Others were J.H. Ross; Wm. Madill; and later, Ditchburn, Hunters, and Dean.

This photo was taken between 1900–1912 at Rolland Boat Palace Livery. Francis Xavier Rolland (standing on the left), George Leacock (standing on the right). (Courtesy of John Rolland)

Rolland Palace Boat Livery, which operated on the waterfront from 1898 to 1966. (Courtesy of John Rolland)

French's Food Stand, while not completed until 1920, became a favourite spot for Stephen Leacock. His table still sits under the overhang each summer, where a plaque commemorates his haunt. Wib and Jean French remember Leacock sitting at the table with his cup of tea. As Wib recalls, tea was served in a china cup and teapot. Leacock would walk up the train track from his home on Old Brewery Bay to the waterfront.

French's Food Stand was right at the water's edge in those days. Over the years, due to the expanded rail beds, infilling changed the shoreline. French's is now back from the water but is still operating each summer.

Depiction of French's Food Stand, where Leacock's table still sits out each summer. (Courtesy of Dale Duncan)

CULTURAL ACTIVITIES

Beyond the businesses identified in *Sunshine Sketches of a Little Town*, there was a wealth of entertainment establishments and cultural activities.

Couchiching Park was a haven for citizens of the town during the warm summers. In 1908 a picnic pavilion was built. This was followed a year later by a bandstand. Designed by W.H. Crocker, architects, these facilities still exist in the park today. Jean French recalls listening to the Kiltie Band play in the bandstand while people sat in the park or listened from boats on the lake.

Couchiching Beach Park on a summer morning. (Leacock Museum Archives)

Orillia boasted three theatres in the early 1900s, the Princess, the Lyceum, and the Crystal Theatre, and they were all located in the downtown area.

The Orillia Opera House was built in 1895 and originally served as a municipal office, lockup, and police office. In 1915 fire destroyed the roof and interior, but reconstruction quickly took place, and by 1917 it was complete. Today the Orillia Opera House still commands attention on the corner of West and Mississaga Streets, serving as a theatre and arts venue.

ALONG THE SHORELINE: HISTORICAL LANDMARKS

The Orillia Opera House is frequented by renowned performers from around the world because of its excellent acoustics.

The Orillia Opera House and market building contained the council chamber and corporate offices. This picture pre-dates the 1919 renovations. This north and east façade view shows the third tower (left), which no longer exists. (Orillia Opera House)

Stephen Leacock's Mariposa

The Orillia Farmers' Market opened on the waterfront of Orillia in the 1840s. The Market moved to the downtown area in 1872 and operated at the same location near the Opera House until 2009, when construction began on the new library. The Market is now located two blocks south on Andrew Street.

The original fire hall is located at 27 Peter Street North. The old fire hall was designed by W.H. Crocker and built in 1896 by J.R. Eaton. It has a magnificent tower for drying hoses and served as a fire hall until 1970, when it was redesigned for offices and apartments.

The former fire hall on Peter Street. (Orillia Public Library)

St. James Court, the site of the original YMCA, is located at 18 Peter Street North. One of the largest YMCA locations in Canada at the time, it was built in 1906 by J.R. Eaton. In 1912 it was the location of the only indoor swimming pool north of Toronto.

The original YMCA. (Leacock Museum Archives)

CHURCHES

In *Sunshine Sketches of a Little Town*, Stephen Leacock focuses on St. James' Anglican Church, but he does make reference to the Baptist, Catholic, Methodist, and Presbyterian churches.

This is a postcard composite photograph of the churches of Orillia. It includes the Baptist church, the Presbyterian church, the Methodist church, the Roman Catholic church, and St. James' Anglican church. (Orillia Public Library)

Historic Residences

The homes of many people characterized in *Sunshine Sketches* still exist today. These historic places can be found in the "older" residential section of Orillia, just north of Mississaga Street. Most of the homes are private residences, although a few are now businesses.

- Dr. Ardagh: 9 Southwood Circle
- Horace Bingham: 160 Peter Street North
- F.G. Evans: 115 Matchedash Street North
- Dr. Gilchrist: 136 Matchedash Street North
- Mr. Thomas Goffatt: 70 Peter Street South, Sir Sam Steele Memorial Building
- Reverend Canon Greene (residence): 57 Neywash Street
- R.D. Gunn: 187 Peter Street North
- John McCosh: 79 West Street North
- McNabb Family (residence): 82 Tecumseth Street
- Mundell Funeral Home (McCosh House): 79 West Street North

Along the Shoreline: Historical Landmarks

The home of Canon Greene (the Rev. Mr. Drone) at 57 Neywash Street, now the Carson Funeral Home reception centre. (Orillia Public Library)

The Champlain Monument, 2012. (Daphne Mainprize)

Chapter Three

The *Sketches*: The Cast of Characters in Leacock's Mariposa

Stephen Leacock bought the property on Old Brewery Bay in 1908. The first summer he pitched a tent, which was followed in subsequent years by the building of a simple cottage along the shoreline. Leacock immersed himself in the life of Orillia and hosted many citizens at his home, "The Old Brewery Bay." He became a familiar figure walking along the shore path to town to sell his vegetables at the Orillia Farmers' Market. He toured the town, dropping in at the barber and bank along the way. In 1928 he completed the nineteen-room cottage that stands on the site today and is now the Stephen Leacock Museum National Historic Site.

When Stephen Leacock wrote *Sunshine Sketches of a Little Town* in 1912, he drew his inspiration from Orillia and the leading citizens of the day. The focus of the book was not to be unkind, but rather he saw himself as one of the local characters and enjoyed living the life of a country gentleman. Leacock's roots came from small town England and Ontario. His imagery in *Sunshine Sketches* represented all that was "good, decent, and eccentric" about rural communities. Leacock left Orillia

The Sketches: The Cast of Characters in Leacock's Mariposa

a legacy from which the town still benefits. This legacy cast a spell over Mariposa, and forever we live in the sunshine with all our "characters" and rural Ontario roots that have come to define the essence of Canada.

Over the past hundred years, Orillia has taken on the mantle of "Mariposa." With the opening of the Stephen Leacock Museum in the 1950s and the designation of the museum as a national historic site in the 1990s, the legacy of Mariposa was cemented for all time as uniquely belonging to Orillia.

Stephen Leacock sailing on Lake Couchiching. (Leacock Museum Archives)

An excerpt from the original manuscript of Sunshine Sketches, *describing Lake Wissanotti at half past six in the morning. (Leacock Museum Archives)*

The Sketches: The Cast of Characters in Leacock's Mariposa

The Islay *on Lake Couchiching under the stewardship of Captain McInnes. (Orillia Public Library)*

The citizens of Mariposa were characterized by Stephen Leacock in *Sunshine Sketches of a Little Town*.

- John Henry Bagshaw, Liberal Candidate
  Based on: Judge R.D. Gunn, Gunn & Ambrose Barristers, or Archie McKinnon, Beaverton

The main street of Orillia at the turn of the century. (Orillia Public Library)

STEPHEN LEACOCK'S MARIPOSA

Couchiching Beach Park in the morning sun. (Leacock Museum Archive)

⊚ Mr. Diston, a high school teacher
  Based on: George Rogers (who later became minister of education)

Orillia District Collegiate Institute. (Leacock Museum Archives)

The Sketches: The Cast of Characters in Leacock's Mariposa

- Reverend Rupert (Dean) Drone, rector, Church of England church
  Based on: Reverend Canon Richard W. Greene, rector, St. James' Anglican Church, 58 Peter Street North

Canon Richard W. Greene, the inspiration for Reverend Drone. (Leacock Museum Archives)

St. James' Anglican Church. (Leacock Museum Archives)

An excerpt from the original manuscript of Sunshine Sketches: Dean Drone. *(Leacock Museum Archives)*

*The Sketches: The Cast of Characters
in Leacock's Mariposa*

The fire at St. James' Anglican Church. (Courtesy of Craig Mainprize)

⊚   George Duff, manager, Mariposa Commercial Bank
    Based on: John Scott, manager, Dominion Bank,
    81–86 Mississaga Street East

The Dominion Bank building. (Orillia Public Library)

STEPHEN LEACOCK'S MARIPOSA

◉ Jim Elliot, proprietor, drug store
   Based on: J.W. Slaven, (Doc) Slaven's Drug Store, 87 Mississaga Street East

Elliot's Drug Store, at the corner of Peter and Mississaga. (Orillia Public Library)

Mr. J. Slaven, the inspiration for Mr. Elliot. (Orillia Public Library)

The Sketches: The Cast of Characters in Leacock's Mariposa

An excerpt from the original manuscript of Sunshine Sketches: *Mr. Elliot. (Leacock Museum Archives)*

- Dr. Gallagher, physician
  Based on: Dr. W.C. Gilchrist or Dr. A.E. Ardagh

Stephen Leacock's Mariposa

Dr. Ardagh, the inspiration for Dr. Gallagher. (Courtesy of Craig Mainprize)

7

Xenophon: And then after that they fell to talking of relics and traces of the past and Dr Gallagher said that ~~he had some indian arrow heads~~ that if Canon Drone would come round to his house some night he would show him some Indian arrow heads that he had dug up in his garden. And Canon Drone said that if Dr Gallagher would come round to the rectory any afternoon he would show him a map of Xerxes invasion of Greece. Only he must come some time between the Infant Class and the Mothers auxiliary. So presently they both knew that they were blocked out of one anothers houses for some time to come, and Dr Gallagher walked forward & told Mr Smith who had never studied Greek about Champlain

An excerpt from the original manuscript of Sunshine Sketches: Dr. Gallagher. *(Leacock Museum Archives)*

*THE SKETCHES: THE CAST OF CHARACTERS
IN LEACOCK'S MARIPOSA*

- Golgotha Gingham, undertaker
  Based on: Horace E. Bingham, undertaker and
  furniture store owner, 141 Mississaga Street East

World Furniture Co., 54 Mississaga Street East, site of Horace E. Bingham's store in 1900. (Orillia Public Library)

4

and his dress was due to the fact that he had just come from ~~an~~ ~~under~~ what he called an "interment". Mr Gingham had the true spirit of his profession ~~and~~ and such words as 'funeral' or 'coffin' or 'hearse' never passed his lips. He spoke always of "interments", of "caskets", and 'coaches', using terms that were calculated rather to bring out the majesty and sublimity of death than to parade its horrors. To be present at the hotel was in accord with Mr Gingham's general conception of his business. No man had ever grasped the true principles of undertaking more thoroughly than Mr Gingham. I have often heard him explain that to associate with the living, uninteresting

An excerpt from the original manuscript of Sunshine Sketches: Golgotha Gingham. *(Leacock Museum Archives)*

The Sketches: The Cast of Characters in Leacock's Mariposa

Mundell Funeral Home. John (Josh) McCosh purchased 79 West Street North in 1887 and constructed the lavish Victorian Gothic mansion that stands today. (Courtesy of Mundell Funeral Home)

- Peter Glover, mayor of Mariposa and proprietor of the hardware store
  Based on: Mr. Leslie Frost

- Mr. Hussell, Mariposa *Newspacket*
  Based on: J. Russell Hale, Orillia *Packet*, 15 Peter Street South
  C. Harold Hale
  George Hughes Hale, Orillia *Packet*
  W. Hale, editor, proprietor, Orillia *Packet*

Stephen Leacock's Mariposa

C. Harold Hale. (Orillia Public Library)

Orillia Packet *was founded in 1870 by W. Hale, who ran it with his brother George C. Harold and his brother Russell (Hussell), George's sons, ran the paper in subsequent years. (Orillia Public Library)*

Excursion boats on Lake Couchiching. (Orillia Public Library)

The Sketches: The Cast of Characters in Leacock's Mariposa

- Henry Mullins, manager, Exchange Bank
  Based on: George Rapley, manager, Traders Bank.
  72–74 Mississaga Street East, Sheppard Block

  Note: Leacock's original manuscript referred to Mullins as George Popley.

Local advertisements in the Packet *paper from 1912, including Traders Bank, with George Rapley, manager. (Orillia Public Library)*

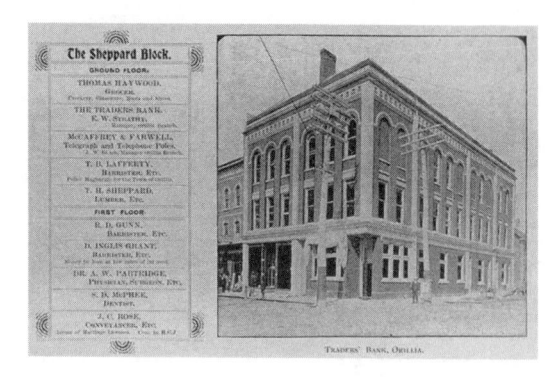

Sheppard Block, the former site of the Traders Bank, offices of Dr. Ardagh, the telegraph office, and J.D. Gunn. (Orillia Public Library)

- Christie Johnson, captain of the *Mariposa Belle*
  Based on: Captain Lachlan (Lockie) Johnston of the steamboat *Enterprise* or Captain Charles McInnes of the steamboat *Islay*, Orillia Wharf

- The *Mariposa Belle* is an amalgam of more than one pleasure boat on Lake Couchiching, but is generally believed to be based on the *Enterprise*.

A sketch of the Enterprise. *(Courtesy of Craig Mainprize)*

The Sketches: The Cast of Characters in Leacock's Mariposa

Mrs. Shaw, Stephen Leacock, and a friend going fishing. (Orillia Public Library)

An excerpt from the original manuscript of Sunshine Sketches: Mariposa Belle. *(Leacock Museum Archives)*

STEPHEN LEACOCK'S MARIPOSA

◉ Macartney, Nivens, barristers
   Based on: F.G. Evans, barrister of the firm McCarthy, Pepler, Evans, and McCarthy. In 1905, Mr. Evans was the president of the Orillia Board of Trade.

The corner of Mississaga and Peter Streets, looking west. (Orillia Public Library)

The home of Mr. Francis G. Evans, the inspiration for lawyers Macartney or Nivens, at 115 Matchedash Street. Mr. Evans was called to the Bar in 1892 and served as a lawyer in Orangeville, Barrie, and Orillia. (Orillia Public Library)

The Sketches: The Cast of Characters in Leacock's Mariposa

An excerpt from the original manuscript of Sunshine Sketches: Nivens. *(Leacock Museum Archives)*

- Ed Moore, photographer
  Based on: B.F. Stewart or E.C. Moore, 133 Mississaga Street East

- Netley, butcher shop and groceries
  Based on: J.J. Hatley, 143–149 Mississaga Street East

The bandstand in Couchiching Park. (Daphne Mainprize)

Hatley's Butcher Shop. (Orillia Public Library)

Inside Hatley's Butcher Shop. (Orillia Public Library)

THE SKETCHES: THE CAST OF CHARACTERS IN LEACOCK'S MARIPOSA

- Judge Pepperleigh, district judge in Missanaba County
  Based on Josh (Joseph McCosh), mayor of Orillia

- Children of Judge Pepperleigh
  Neil Pepperleigh: based on Percy McCosh
  Zena Pepperleigh: based on Gwen or Ouida McCosh

An excerpt from the original manuscript of Sunshine Sketches: *Jos. Smith. (Leacock Museum Archives)*

Mr. John McCosh, mayor of Orillia on several occasions and police magistrate. Inspiration for Judge Pepperleigh. (Orillia Public Library)

- Peter Pupkin, bank teller, Exchange Bank
  Based on: Jack Stevens of Traders Bank

- Jos. Smith, proprietor, Jos. Smith Hostelry
  Based on: Jim Smith, proprietor of the Daly House, 157–159 Mississaga Street East

The hotel operated by Jos. Smith is an amalgam of several, including the Orillia Hotel, the Albion Hotel (Chris Moore), and the Daly House. The Daly House is generally attributed to the Jos. Smith Hostelry. (Orillia Public Library)

THE SKETCHES: THE CAST OF CHARACTERS IN LEACOCK'S MARIPOSA

An excerpt from the original manuscript of Sunshine Sketches: *George Popley (later changed to Henry Mullins). (Leacock Museum Archives)*

Stephen Leacock's Mariposa

- Jefferson Thorpe, barber
  Based on: Jeff Shortt, barber, 156b Mississaga Street East

- Myra Thorpe (wife of Jefferson)
  Based on: Minerva Shortt (wife of Jeff)

An excerpt from the original manuscript of Sunshine Sketches: *Jefferson Thorpe. (Leacock Museum Archives)*

The Sketches: The Cast of Characters in Leacock's Mariposa

- Mallory Tompkins, proprietor, *Times-Herald* newspaper
  Based on: Unknown, possibly a compilation of the Hale brothers

Orillia Times *newspaper. (Orillia Public Library)*

STEPHEN LEACOCK'S MARIPOSA

- Alf Trelawney, postmaster
  Based on: George Thomson or Thomas Goffatt of 30 Peter Street South

Post office. The Sir Sam Steele Building, 1900, now the Orillia Museum of Art and History. (Orillia Museum of Art and History)

Thomas Goffatt, postmaster. (Orillia Public Library)

78

The Sketches: The Cast of Characters in Leacock's Mariposa

OTHER CHARACTERS

- Mr. Dreery, high-school English literature teacher
- Lilian Drone, wife of Canon Dean Drone
- Fizzlechip, teacher
- Will Harrison, harness maker
- Miss Lawson, high school teacher
- Peter McGinnis, Liberal organizer
- Joe Milligan, dentist
- Alf McNicol, paint store owner
- Bill Rawson, telegraph operator
- Pete Robinson, Continental Hotel proprietor
- Mr. Uttermost (curate), based on Reverend Longfeldt
- Yodel (auctioneer), Jim Slater
- Miss Cleghorn, telephone exchange
- Miss Spiffkins, biology teacher, high school
- Mr. Muddleston, principal, high school
- Gillis, caretaker at Exchange Bank of Mariposa
- Alphonse (Alf) French chef, Smith's Hotel
- Drone girls: Lilian, Jocelyn, and Theodora
- Edward Drone, the dean's younger brother
- Billy, desk clerk, Smith's Hotel

STEPHEN LEACOCK'S MARIPOSA

Passengers on an excursion on Lake Couchiching. (Orillia Public Library)

Stephen Leacock. (Courtesy of Craig Mainprize)

Chapter Four
Mariposa Citizens Today

One hundred years later, the incarnation of Mariposa that Stephen Leacock created in *Sunshine Sketches of a Little Town* embodies Orillia. Now a bustling city, "The Sunshine City," with a population of over 30,000, is still defined by the Leacock legacy, and the gold dust Stephen Leacock sprinkled over the people and place that is Mariposa still glistens today. Orillia is forever Mariposa, shimmering in the sunshine.

What impact did the writing of *Sunshine Sketches of a Little Town* have on Orillia over the past hundred years? What is the legacy Stephen Leacock left the city?

Mariposans of today have some thoughts about the above questions. They live and work in similar occupations as the characters Stephen Leacock wrote about. Do they identify with the characters out of *Sunshine Sketches*? Let's find out in their own words.

Mayor Angelo Orsi, City of Orillia

Orillia has a leg-up on other towns and cities by virtue of Stephen Leacock's *Sunshine Sketches of a Little Town*.

Angelo Orsi. (Courtesy of Angelo Orsi)

The warmth and jovial nature of the book brings people to our city expecting a warm welcome and a friendly smile, and that's what Orillians are best known for.

In an economy where so much depends on our ability to welcome people and make them feel included, Leacock has laid a terrific foundation for us. Today we might call it customer service or community relations, but just by starting with a warm, friendly, and welcoming attitude, we're halfway there.

So much in Orillia is linked to Stephen Leacock and *Sunshine Sketches*. Its place names live on as names of local businesses and organizations, whether it's "*Sunshine Sketches*" this or "*Brewery Bay*" that, including my own family business, Mariposa Homes.

I like the part where Mariposa mayor Pete Glover, of Glover's Hardware and Paint, virtually splits his business in half over politics. As soon as there was an election, Mr. Glover, a Conservative, sold hardware on one side of the store and his partner, Alf McNicol, a Liberal, sold paint on the other.

And don't forget, Leacock's Judge Pepperleigh was based on former Orillia mayor John McCosh, who served for five terms. Mayor McCosh had a keen eye for real estate and developed many parcels of land, including building the Syndicate Block downtown, which housed the barbershop of Jeff Shortt, known in *Sunshine Sketches* as barber Jefferson Thorpe.

There's lots to like about Leacock and *Sunshine Sketches*, and it all starts with good-natured humour and friendly people who always mean well and can be counted on to pitch in for any community cause. In that way, Orillia and Mariposa will always be connected.

Reverend Terry Bennett

The Reverend Drone is based on the "real life" character of the Reverend Canon Richard Greene, rector of St. James' Anglican Church, Orillia, from 1868 to 1911.

Stephen Leacock may have known him as a "droning" cleric in the pulpit. He was probably educated in the classical tradition of Anglican clergy. Bright and articulate, he may have lacked the common touch for the people of Orillia, or "Mariposa."

Reverend Terry Bennett. (Courtesy of Terry Bennett)

The Reverend Greene sculpted the eagle lectern at St. James' Church (the eagle representing "truth"). He also taught Franklin Carmichael to paint and produced many beautiful watercolours that hang in the present-day rectory. His lengthy stay in Orillia allowed Stephen Leacock to sit before his pulpit every Sunday. The front pew on the left side bears a marker dedicated to Mr. Leacock, who was known to sit there on Sunday morning looking up and occasionally checking his pocket watch.

The Reverend Dean Drone haunts the memory of all clergy of St. James' Church. He reminds us that we can easily become caught up in our role and therefore irrelevant to life around us.

I read *Sunshine Sketches of a Little Town* before

arriving in Orillia. I laughed through much of the book. But upon my arrival, I discovered many of the elder Orillians were not amused. Whether the facts were based on half-truths or total fabrications, many felt Orillia had been smeared as a small Ontario town.

I never thought about it very seriously. Like many humorists, Stephen Leacock was simply poking fun at the fallible institutions and people in a small town. The town could be anywhere in this province and the figures would have remained the same.

Dean Drone was the rector of the Anglican church. Those of us who are clergy are not offended by his character in *Sunshine Sketches of a Little Town*. He appears, like many of the characters, without the many dimensions of a real person. He would seem to be so "heaven bound" and academic that he is no earthly use to anyone. The reverend gentleman is the caricature of an "old time" parson, and he serves that purpose. I can laugh at Dean Drone, as some aspects of his person are true of all clergy.

The Stephen Leacock Museum has drawn people from all over to its doors. Just when we thought that Stephen Leacock was disappearing from the literary and historical scene, he has found new life. The rebirth of his reputation and writing should be embraced by Orillia. The "Mariposa" he wrote of still exists in many aspects of our lives. It has been fortunate for us here in Orillia.

STEVE CLARKE, PROPRIETOR, BREWERY BAY FOOD COMPANY

Steve Clarke. (Courtesy of Steve Clarke)

I believe that Stephen Leacock's image has truly evolved over the decades. This is partly because of some of his alleged habits, but more due to the images he created of a number of key Orillians. It was *Sunshine Sketches* that led to Leacock's vilification, which continued into at least the 1940s and '50s. This was probably best evidenced when, many years after his death, and his success worldwide, the Orillia city council voted against sending a copy of *Sunshine Sketches* to the queen, still harbouring some resentment towards Leacock. Stephen

Leacock has been embraced by the community at large, but has still not received his due recognition!

Although there has been a slow change in the local attitude toward Leacock, there is much more work to be done. I say this primarily for two reasons. First, I believe that Leacock has never really received the local recognition that is merited by his international success. Second, and perhaps from somewhat selfish motives, I believe we need to tap into the legacy of Leacock and take that to the next level. Orillia has in its midst a marketing tool that few communities can boast of, or even dream about. Stratford and Niagara-on-the-Lake had to import the names of William Shakespeare and George Bernard Shaw respectively. Orillia has been blessed with the talented and globally successful Mr. Leacock. There has been some wonderful work and some results over the years, but with strategic partnerships between culture, education, business, and the city, the opportunities to elevate Leacock and the City of Orillia are limitless!

I have heard the Jos. Smith comparison to myself a number of times over the years. Each time, of course, it was very "tongue-in-cheek"! If I or my business have made any recognizable contribution to the community, I hope that it's for slightly contrasting reasons. Although these are indeed different times, Mr. "Smith," for example, appears to have an altered regard for the laws surrounding the service of alcohol. I have truly enjoyed my first nineteen years as a "hostilier" in the Sunshine City of Mariposa, but many of the comparisons stop there. As *Maclean's* magazine recently noted (in Leacockian fashion), our different body types and my being a vegetarian disqualify me from further comparison. I would hope that if Leacock were alive and writing today, I might have done something notorious over the years to be worthy of his wit. Alas, I fear that, unlike the thinly masked Mr. Smith, I have led far too mundane an existence to be worthy.

Doug Downey, Lawyer with Lewis, Downey, Tornosky, Lassaline, and Timpano

Doug Downey. (Courtesy of Doug Downey)

The impact of *Sunshine Sketches* must at the time have been a relief for those not skewered, and a source of righteous indignation to those who were. Ironically, vanity would have made being named more desirable than not.

It was the lampooning of a whole city that at times took itself seriously. As time passed, I believe the story was embraced as a clever insight into human nature, regardless of the setting.

Orillia was confident and self-deprecating enough to capture the opportunity presented to it through the broad appeal of *Sunshine Sketches*.

Lawyer Macartney is an important but minor character in the story. Leacock largely avoids picking on lawyers — it is not clever enough for him. Although he goes after politicians, he avoids the other low-hanging fruit. In his later works, he can't restrain himself.

People watch Macartney to see when spring will start, like a groundhog with tennis shorts. He is involved in the whirlwind campaign and shows up whenever there is something to be done, as does everyone.

In our Orillia, the lawyers are often leaders and not just attendees of sub-groups (YMCA, Doug Christie; OSMH Foundation, Hon. Doug Lewis). I think there is greater community involvement by the Bar than just socializing with judges inside (or being locked out of) the bar.

I identify with Macartney to the extent that he is fortunate to hold a respectable position in society because of his education and training.

The Leacock legacy spans time. It is an insight into our past, as humans and Orillians. It is in the present, as citizens often say, "If Leacock were to write *Sunshine Sketches* today ..." and then they shake their heads at some decision that has been made. It is a measure, a prism, and a mirror for current events here in Orillia. It is also an opportunity to build future value for Orillia. The more distant in time we are from the original writing, the easier it is to understand that "the more things change, the more they stay the same."

We are fortunate Leacock thought enough about us to gift us the legacy of his wit and insight.

Mark Fletcher, Professor, Georgian College

Mark Fletcher. (Courtesy of Mark Fletcher)

I am, even by Orillia standards, a relative newcomer to the town. My family was part of the waves of Scottish immigrants to settle in Oro in the mid-1800s. I sensed at an early age that Orillia was considered the "centre of the universe" by most Orillians.

I think this is linked to the physical charm of the city and unquestionably to the historic Leacock connection to our community.

My understanding is that the "centre of the universe" thinking began in Leacock's day, and it manifests itself in many ways, the most noticeable being that, ever since those days, many of our citizens, both elected and non-elected, have had a majestic dose of hubris and a certain "mojo" that at times is breathtaking and hilarious, in true Leacock fashion.

TOM GOSTICK, ISLAND PRINCESS BOAT CRUISES

Captain Tom Gostick. (Courtesy of Tom Gostick)

Island Princess. *(Courtesy of Tom Gostick)*

I suppose the *Enterprise* was one of the many boats on the lake, of course, but my research always sends me in the direction of Captain McInnes and the *Islay* when the *Mariposa Belle* is brought into the conversation.

It really was the only boat with the capacity to take "crowds" on cruises, and it had electrical lights and a piano, so it was the party boat. Additionally, Captain McInnes had the only liquor licence in the area, on Strawberry Island. When it came to cruises, he was your man.

Captain McInnes's career spanned about twenty-five years. Right now I am in my twenty-ninth season.

Orillia is "Leacock," the same as Niagara-on-the-Lake is "Shaw." The very identifiable characters in *Sunshine Sketches* were only to the benefit of Orillia. Our fellow was very funny! Everyone enjoys a good laugh, right?

We are the Sunshine City, and just watching the local weather out of Barrie, you will hear Bob say "and for your friends up there in the Sunshine City," so what more could you ask for? It's our identity. I really do get upset when I hear folks taking us in other directions, trying to "brand" us.

The sketches truly drew blood with the locals. Even to this day some of Leacock's comical characters in real life hold a grudge. Although his initials were SBL (Stephen Butler Leacock), most folks back then and even today still call him that old SOB! They didn't like being the subject of his humour.

JOHN HAMMILL, PUBLISHER, ORILLIA PACKET *AND* TIMES

John Hammill. (Courtesy of Farzin Photography)

Throughout Lake Country there are many settings of historical significance, and the Stephen Leacock Museum is certainly one of the jewels that belongs at the top of the list. I understand *Sunshine Sketches* was not originally received all that well and was seen as offensive by some locals. Obviously, time has dramatically changed that perception, and with the Leacock museum being designated a national historic site, I think Orillians can be very proud that the dawn of Canadian humour can be traced back to the Sunshine City.

As the local newspaper of record, it doesn't matter if we are reporting on tourism activities across Lake Country, city council meetings, or even the price of hogs in Mariposa — providing accurate, trustworthy content will always be our goal, so yes, I can identify with Mr. Hussell and the challenges he would have faced.

I would imagine Mr. Hussell and his team would have a difficult time getting into Jos. Smith's backroom on a regular basis back then. Could you imagine if all the mugwumps in Mariposa had the use of the *Packet*'s modern-day blog? Users might have helped Mr. Pupkin with his relationship issues, or the online community could have helped the Mariposa stuffed shirts actually complete their whirlwind campaign and even save time by doing it online!

The only advice I would dare offer to Mr. Hussell and his team would be to please double-check the dispatch; the last thing the *Newspacket* needs to be known for is a candidate Jos. C. Smith calamity.

Orillia is fortunate to have many defining

characteristics: the Champlain Monument, the Opera House, our beautiful vistas, and we have *Sunshine Sketches of a Little Town* as our literary landmark. Orillians are hard-working people, and I'm certain the spirit of Mariposa's Mr. Smith and the like are alive and well here today.

Sunshine Sketches reminds us that no matter how hard we work, it's important to find time to celebrate the simple things in life.

Chapter Five

Stephen Leacock Museum National Historic Site

By Fred Addis, curator, Stephen Leacock Museum

Since the museum was first opened as the Stephen Leacock Memorial Home in 1958, Orillia has been joined at the hip with the life and legacy of Stephen Butler Leacock. In this jubilee year of his classic *Sunshine Sketches of a Little Town*, it is nearly impossible to think about Orillia without referencing Leacock and his beloved Mariposa.

As the person who is paid to take Leacock seriously, it is an almost daily struggle for me to maintain some degree of perspective between Leacock the historical figure and Leacock the humorist. Indeed, the two are nearly inseparable.

Very early in my tenure, a visiting author accused Orillia of having built a shrine to Leacock and therefore being unable to hear anything other than the most positive interpretation of his life and work.

But put anyone in Orillia on a pedestal, and five minutes later someone will knock him off with a story of outrageous or mean-spirited behaviour, true or not.

I like to say that we interpret Stephen Leacock in all his complexities: from the depths of his personal and family tragedies, to the heights of the master humorist at the top of his craft, and everywhere in between.

With an actual shrine to real-life martyrs just down the road in Midland, we in Orillia must be measured in our veneration of Leacock and perhaps be careful of lapsing into hyperbole. You don't have to worship Stephen Leacock to appreciate his humour. You needn't speak of him using terms such as "greatest" or "funniest." Stephen Leacock is remarkable for his achievement in two professional camps: academics and humour. Surprising and unlikely bedfellows, some might say, but each the richer for the other.

One hundred years after its publication, *Sunshine Sketches* still resonates with its readers, young and old, all the while challenging our vision of ourselves and our community. There is a comfortable and friendly hand at work throughout. It is the hand of a masterful writer writing about people and places he knew intimately.

On a personal note, I encountered Stephen Leacock for the first time at the age of ten. I was given some extra reading by my teacher, and the assigned piece was title, "The Sinking of the *Mariposa Belle*," as *The Marine Excursion of the Knights of Pythias* was often known. I remember laughing out loud, thereby defeating my teacher's objective of keeping me both busy and quiet.

Longevity, from the point of view of readership and public appreciation, is the mark of artistic accomplishment. And there is every indication that a hundred years from now, in whatever form, readers will still be discovering Stephen Leacock and his uniquely Canadian sense of humour.

Stephen Leacock Museum National Historic Site. (Leacock Museum Archives)

The actor Gordon Pinsent (left), who played Stephen Leacock in the CBC TV's production of Sunshine Sketches of a Little Town, *which aired in February 2012, is shown with Leacock Museum curator Fred Addis. (Courtesy of D. Campeau)*

The original cottage on the shores of Old Brewery Bay. (Leacock Museum Archives)

Stephen Leacock in his skiff at the boathouse. (Leacock Museum Archives)

Chapter Six

The Walking Tour of Stephen Leacock's Mariposa

The Walking Tour

As you leave the lakeshore you will be directed to the walking trail (original CPR track).

1. Stephen Leacock Museum National Historic Site, Museum Drive. This national historic site is the summer home of Stephen Butler Leacock.

2. Former Jackson's Brewery. Stephen Leacock named his home "The Old Brewery Bay."

3. Train Station. The trail takes you to the waterfront of Mariposa. To your left is the original station (now the Royal Canadian Legion).

4. Former Rolland Palace Boat Livery. On your right is the site where several boat liveries existed. The Rolland boat livery operated from 1898 to 1966.

5. *Mariposa Belle*. On your right is the dock where the *Mariposa Belle* was moored (now *Island Princess*).

6. Bandstand. As you make your way along the boardwalk into the park, you will see the bandstand, built in 1909.

7. Picnic Pavilion. Behind the bandstand and built in 1908.

8. Champlain Monument. Directly in front of the picnic pavilion.

9. French's Food Stand. This is where Leacock took tea on summer afternoons.

Mariposa Main Street. As you leave the park, you will make your way up the right (north) side of the main street.

10. Jeff Thorpe Barber Shop, 156b Mississaga Street East (Bodyco)

11. Dominion Bank, 82–86 Mississaga Street East (Pizza Pizza)

Turn right onto Peter Street North

12. Former YMCA, 18 Peter Street North (St. James' Court)

13. St. James' Anglican Church, 58 Peter Street North

14. Original Fire Hall, 27 West Street North (offices)

Return to Mississaga Street East and turn right

15. Sheppard Block, 72–78 Mississaga Street East, location of Traders Bank, Dr. Ardagh, telegraph office, and J.D. Gunn office (Accura Business Centre).

16. *Times-Herald* office, 64 Mississaga Street East (Royal LePage Real Quest Realty)

17. Orillia Hotel, 38–42 Mississaga Street East

Turn right onto West Street North

18. Judge Pepperleigh's House, 79 West Street North (Mundell Funeral Home)

19. Orillia Town Office and Lockup, 35 West Street North (offices)

20. Orillia Opera House, 20 Mississaga Street West

Turn right onto Mississaga Street West

21. Orillia Public Library. 36 Mississaga Street West site of the former Carnegie Library

22. Site of the former Farmer's Market

Cross over to the south side of Mississaga Street West

23. Wright's Brewery, 39–37 Mississaga Street West (Fred's Meat Market)

24. Frost Jewellery, 51 Mississaga Street East (Town's Jewellery)

25. MacNab's Hardware, 61–63 Mississaga Street East

Turn right onto Peter Street South

26. Orillia *Newsletter*, 11–13 Peter Street South (Zephyr Art Gallery)

27. *Packet* Office, 15 Peter Street South (Shadowbox Art Gallery)

Cross over at Colborne Street S. (South side of Peter Street South)

The Walking Tour of Stephen Leacock's Mariposa

28. Post Office, Peter Street South (Orillia Museum of Art & History)

Turn right onto Mississaga Street East

29. Slaven's Drug Store, 83 Mississaga Street East

30. Moore's Liquor Store, 87 Mississaga Street East

31. Stewart's Photographs, 105 Mississaga Street East (Seasons Shop)

32. Geo. Vick Grocery, 109–119 Mississaga Street East (Mariposa Market) (Brewery Bay Food Company)

33. Chris Moore General Store, 133 Mississaga Street East (Tre Sorelle)

34. Horace E. Bingham, undertaker, 141 Mississaga Street East (Saturday Afternoons)

35. Hatley's Grocery and Butcher, 143–149 Mississaga Street East(Jack & Maddy: A Kid's Store) (Tor's Fish & Chip)

36. Daly House (Russell House), 157–159 Mississaga Street East

37. Robinson's Continental, 175 Mississaga St. E. (Kahuna Surf Shop)

STEPHEN LEACOCK'S MARIPOSA

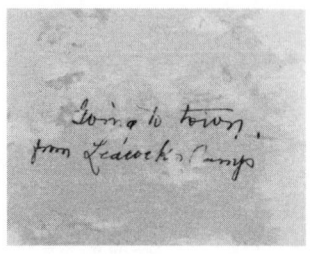

Going to town from Leacock's Camp. (Orillia Public Library)

Stephen Leacock fishing. (Orillia Public Library)

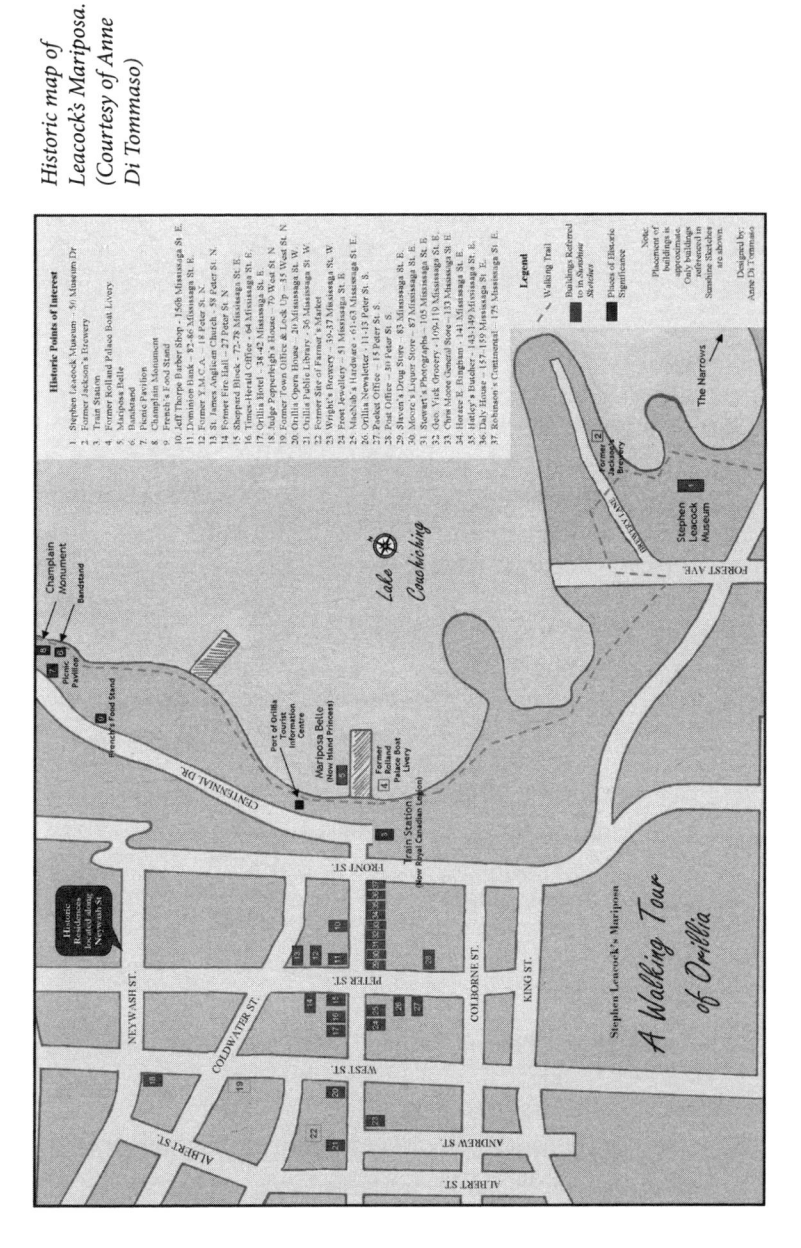

Historic map of Leacock's Mariposa. (Courtesy of Anne Di Tommaso)

Sources

Chapter One

"Things to Know About Orillia," *The News Letter*, February 21, 1912, 1.

Stephen Leacock, *Letter to His Mother*, May 30, 1907 (Leacock Museum Archives).

Chapter Two

Conversation with John Rolland, 2012.

Conversation with Wib and Jean French, 2012.

Chapters Three and Six

Stephen Leacock, *Sunshine Sketches of a Little Town*, edited by Carl Spadoni (Broadview Press, 2002), Appendix C (Sunshine Sketches and Orillia), 178–81.

Memories of Mississaga Street taken from *Memories of Late 1880s & 1890s*, compiled by M. Teefy Mulcahy, April 1960, drawn by Shirley Tapp (Orillia Public Library).

SOURCES

Conversation with Ralph Cipolla, 2012.

Conversation with Wendy Hutchings and Marcel Rousseau, Orillia Museum of Art and History, 2012.

Helen Raposo, City of Orillia, 2012.

Websites of Interest

For readers interested in additional information about subjects covered in this book, please see the following websites.

- Stephen Leacock Museum
    www.leacockmuseum.com/
- Mnjikaning Fish Weirs
    www.historicplaces.ca/en/rep-reg/place-lieu.aspx?id=9679
- The History of Simcoe County
    www.waynecook.com/hunter2.shtml
- Champlain Monument
    http://en.wikipedia.org/wiki/Vernon_March
- Mariposa
    http://en.wikipedia.org/wiki/Mariposa_(fictional_town)
- The Lands Between
    www.thelandbetween.ca/about.asp
- Orillia Opera House
    http://orilliaoperahouse.ca/
- Dale Duncan
    www.cellarart.ca

Websites of Interest

- Orillia Farmers' Market
  www.orilliafarmersmarket.on.ca

- Ontario Lake Country
  www.ontariolakecountry.com

- Downtown Orillia
  www.downtownorillia.org

- City of Orillia
  www.orillia.com

- Orillia Museum of Art & History
  www.orilliamuseum.org

MIX
Paper from
responsible sources
FSC® C004071